# Getting AFLOAT

*All you need to know about starting to sail small boats*

## BASIL MOSENTHAL
## with Sue Pelling

With an Introduction by
Ben Ainslie

Adlard Coles Nautical
London

# COME SAILING!

### Because sailing is fun - and it's even more fun if you learn to sail well.

But what can you learn from a book? This one will help you in two ways:

- ☐ First, if you haven't sailed before, it will tell you how easy it is to get started.

  Although you can't learn to sail entirely from a book, this one will help you while you are being taught. For instance, it will tell you the names for the various parts of a boat and the sails, and some of the many other new words and expressions that you will come across when you are sailing.

- ☐ Second, it is a handy pocket reference book (which will fit nicely in your sailing bag) which contains information on important things like the tide, the weather, and how to tie knots.

  Then there is advice about dinghy racing and a simple explanation of some of the racing rules, because the chances are that you will find yourself taking part in races with other new sailors very soon after you start sailing.

  And finally, you can find out about charts and buoys, about the flags that other boats are flying, about exploring in a dinghy, and how to progress to sailing in bigger boats.

  Although learning to sail a boat is the first and most important part of getting afloat, you will also want to understand what is going on around you on the water.

**So get afloat, and start enjoying yourself.**

# FOREWORD

**1995** RYA Youth Champion
Laser Class

**1995** ISAF World Youth Champion
Laser Class

**1996** Olympic Silver Medallist
Laser Class

**1999** World Champion Laser Class

*There has never been a better time to get afloat and start sailing. There are so many clubs, so many places to learn, and so many exciting boats to sail.*

*You will probably start in a simple boat – which can still be lots of fun. But if you find that you enjoy sailing and racing, become ambitious. Get your boat set up right, watch what is going on, and learn to race well.*

*Even if you don't have a boat, remember that in a two-handed boat an expert helmsman needs a good crew, and that could be you. So go for it! Get afloat and learn all you can. But remember that you don't have to be a champion to enjoy sailing.*

*Ben Ainslie*

## Acknowledgements

Chart extracts are reproduced by kind permission of the Controller, H. M. Stationery Office and the Hydrographer of the Navy.

**Photographs**
Photographs in this book are reproduced by courtesy of: – Tom Benn (cover); Ben Ainslie page 3; Sue Pelling pages 6, 14 (*Comet Duo*), 15 (*Snipe*); Peter Bentley pages 14 (*Int. 14*), 15 (*Europe*); Topper International page 14 (*Spice*); Musto Ltd & Kos Photos pages 26, 27; LDC Racing Sailboats pages 8, 9, 15 (*RS200*); Yachts & Yachting page 14 (*Spice*); Sailboat & Windsurf page 15 (*Buzz*); Chris Baker pages 15 (*Wayfarer*), 31, 66; Roger Lean-Vercoe page 43; John Goode page 73

**Illustrations**
Robert Mathias

Published 2000 by Adlard Coles Nautical
an imprint of A & C Black (Publishers) Ltd
35 Bedford Row, London WC1R 4JH

ISBN 0-7136-5278-0

A CIP catalogue record of this book is available from the British Library.

Design direction: Robert Mathias
Designer: Helen Mathias
Typeset in 13/15pt Caslon 725 by
Robert Mathias, Publishing Workshop.

Printed and bound in Singapore
through Printlink International Co

# CONTENTS

CHAPTER 1

# HOW TO GET STARTED

## WHERE?

There are sailing clubs in almost every harbour and estuary around the coast, and there are also many schools and sailing centres where you can learn to sail.

But you do not have to live near the sea to start sailing. There are also sailing clubs and sailing centres on many rivers, lakes and reservoirs too.

△ Club members get their boats ready for a day's sailing.

There are even some places where you can sail on a flooded gravel pit. So wherever you live there will be somewhere not too far away where you can learn to sail. Why not check out the Internet.

## HOW?

One way to take up sailing is at a sailing club, and many clubs arrange courses for young sailors especially during the school holidays. In some places there are sailing centres run by local authorities, and there are also many commercial sailing schools.

Whatever you choose, it is generally better to pick somewhere that is approved by the RYA because it will be well organised and have properly

 The Royal Yachting Association (RYA) is keen to help you get started, and you can obtain a list of recommended sailing clubs, schools and sailing centres from them to help you find one near to where you live. The RYA are at

RYA House, Romsey Road, Eastleigh, Hampshire SO50 9YA
Telephone 01703 627400.
Or visit the RYA website www.rya.org.uk

qualified instructors. This means that you will be well taught and will be able to enjoy yourself more.

## THEN...

Learning to sail is a progressive business, and you will probably start off in a simple boat. You will be taught how to rig her ready for sailing, and how to launch her, before taking your first steps afloat.

This book will tell you the things you will want to learn as you progress as a sailor.

You do not have to race when you go sailing, but it is a good way to learn and almost everyone enjoys it. So you may soon be able to join in races with others who are also learning.

You may well learn to sail in a single-handed dinghy, although most small boats need a crew of two. But you can learn a lot by crewing for others. Any helmsman is glad of a good crew, and you can get just as much pleasure from crewing as you can from helming – especially during races.

▷ The **Topper** is a very popular single-handed dinghy. It is easy to handle and also very fast.

## CLOTHING

When you go sailing you will find that you will almost certainly get your feet and legs wet. And although it may be a fine day ashore, it can be much colder on the water if you are not properly dressed. Initially you can start off with warm trousers and a lightweight waterproof jacket.

Although you may need some special clothing for sailing, don't be tempted to splash out until you have seen what other sailors are wearing. Choose the clothes you prefer and which you find the most comfortable.

Many regular dinghy sailors like a close-fitting neoprene wetsuit which keeps the body warm when they get wet and is also not too bulky. A spray top or all-in-one lightweight overall worn over a wetsuit will not only keep the wind out, but will also protect it from getting damaged.

If you are at a sailing school you may find that you can borrow a wetsuit.

Once you have really got into dinghy sailing, you will probably want to invest in a drysuit. Although more expensive than a basic wetsuit, a drysuit will, as the name implies, keep you dry, and if cared for properly, it will last for years.

△ Dinghy boots will keep your feet warm and dry.

### YOUR FEET

One of the most important items of sailing clothing is footwear. There are lots of options on the market, but for your first time out on the water, a pair of non-slip trainer-type shoes will be fine (although they should not be too heavy). Some of the best sailing boots on the market are made of neoprene wetsuit material. They have non-slip soles and help to keep your feet warm when they are wet.

☐ Do not, however, be tempted to sail in bare feet, even if it is summertime. Apart from the obvious risk of getting cold feet, you will find that you *will* knock or cut your feet and this could ruin your day's sailing.

### GLOVES AND HATS

Special sailing gloves are not essential for your first time on the water, but once you have 'learnt the ropes' a pair of sailing gloves can be a good option. They will help you grip the lines and will keep your hands warm in winter.

On a chilly day afloat a hat or cap is a great help in keeping you warm. Attach a safety cord to your cap to stop it blowing away.

▷ Remove your gloves for tying knots and doing up shackles – it is easier. Or buy fingerless gloves like these.

▷ Even if you can swim quite well, you will have to wear a lifejacket or buoyancy aid (see Chapter 5). These are often supplied by the school or club, but in time you may want to buy your own. Once again, get advice.

### GLASSES
If you wear sunglasses or ordinary spectacles, make sure you secure them with a safety cord. They are easily blown off when you are out on the water.

CHAPTER 2

# SAILORS' TALK

**What things are called in boats.**

Your instructor will show you your boat, but before you can launch it, you'll have to learn how to rig it. That is, you'll have to put all the bits together and get the boat ready to sail.

There are quite a few names and sailing terms to learn about boats that you do not find ashore. But this language is easily picked up and you will soon be using it without thinking. The same terms will apply to any boat that you sail.

▷ *A typical sailing dinghy. It can be made either of wood or plastic.*

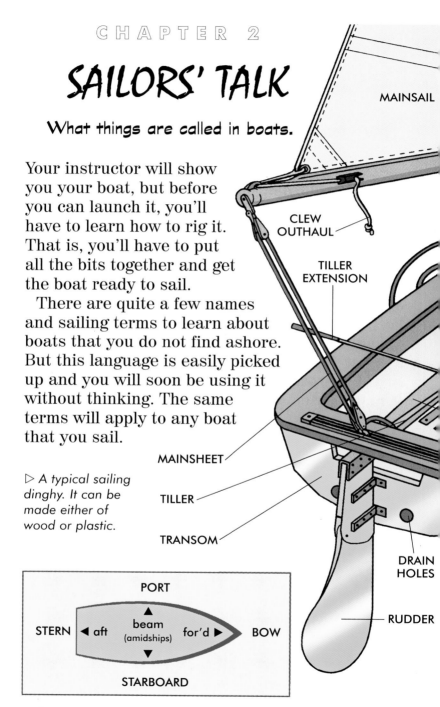

MAINSAIL

CLEW OUTHAUL

TILLER EXTENSION

MAINSHEET

TILLER

TRANSOM

DRAIN HOLES

RUDDER

PORT

STERN ◀ aft — beam (amidships) — for'd ▶ BOW

STARBOARD

△ *Directions in a boat and on the sea are different from those ashore.*

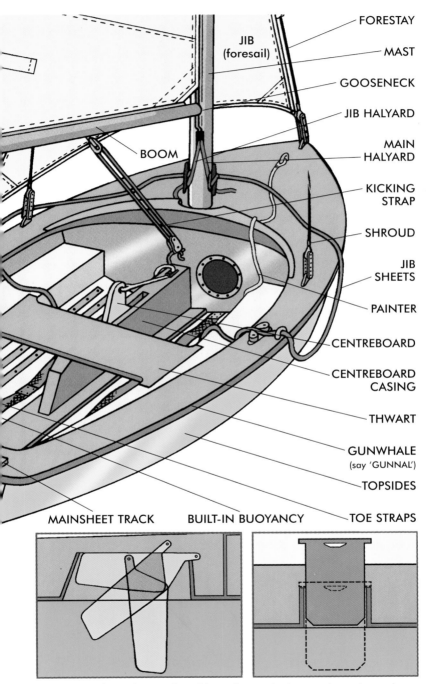

FORESTAY

MAST

GOOSENECK

JIB HALYARD

MAIN HALYARD

KICKING STRAP

SHROUD

JIB SHEETS

PAINTER

CENTREBOARD

CENTREBOARD CASING

THWART

GUNWHALE (say 'GUNNAL')

TOPSIDES

TOE STRAPS

JIB (foresail)

BOOM

MAINSHEET TRACK

BUILT-IN BUOYANCY

△ A centreboard is a plate hinged at one corner that can be raised or lowered.

△ A dagger board can be raised or lowered through a slot built into the hull.

The names of many things on a boat will not change, whatever its size. A mainsheet is still a mainsheet, whether it is on a tiny *Optimist* dinghy or a large cruising yacht – it is just a matter of scale.

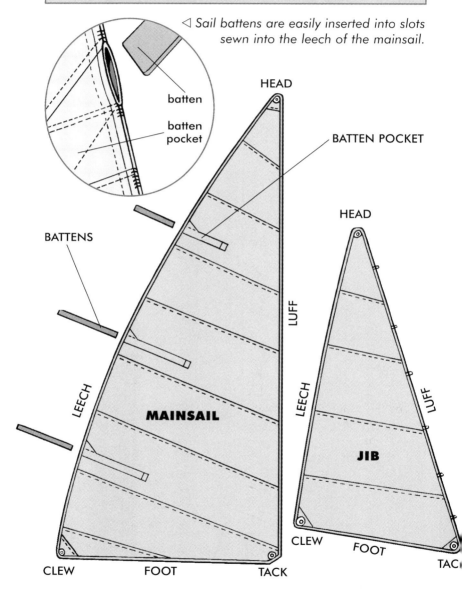

◁ *Sail battens are easily inserted into slots sewn into the leech of the mainsail.*

batten

batten pocket

HEAD

BATTEN POCKET

HEAD

BATTENS

LUFF

LEECH

LEECH

LUFF

**MAINSAIL**

**JIB**

CLEW

FOOT

TACK

CLEW

FOOT

TAC

△ *These are the sails typically used on a small sailing dinghy. The mainsail normally has two or three battens to stiffen it and maintain its shape. The foresail does not usually have any battens.*

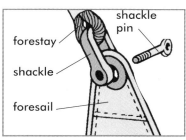

△ Attaching the jib halyard to the head of the foresail.

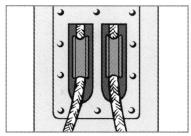

△ Dinghy halyards often run down the inside of the mast.

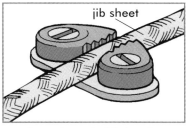

△ Clam cleats hold the jib sheets firmly but they can also be released very quickly.

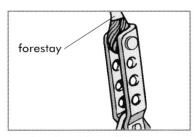

△ The shrouds and forestay are attached to the main dinghy hull with shroud plates.

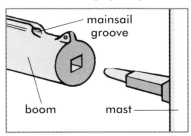

△ The gooseneck is a simple method of attaching the boom to the mast.

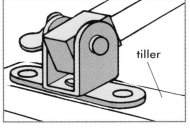

△ The swivel attachment of the detachable tiller extension.

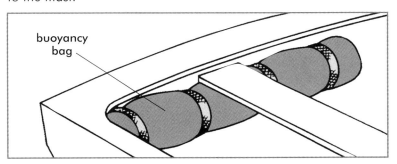

△ Some dinghies have separate inflatable buoyancy bags. They should be well secured so they don't float away during a capsize.

CHAPTER 3

# SOME BOATS YOU WILL SEE AND SAIL

△ Comet Duo

△ Laser (Pico)

△ Spice

△ International 14

△ Buzz

△ RS200

△ Snipe

△ Wayfarer

△ Europe

CHAPTER 4

# GETTING GOING

### Rigging and launching your boat - and de-rigging it when you return to the shore.

Your first sailing lessons will be on how to rig your boat and how to launch it into the water. The drill will vary slightly according to the type of dinghy, and the local conditions. Your instructor will show you the proper way to do it and get you started. In fact, for your first couple of sailing trips, someone experienced is likely to be in the boat with you.

## STARTING OUT

**DO** – have a good look at the pictures in the last chapter – *Sailors' Talk* - before you start. You will see from the illustrations the names for the parts of your boat and its gear. Of course the layout of different dinghies may vary, but the basic equipment will be the same.

**DO** – change into your sailing gear before you start so that the rigged boat is not left unattended. Make sure you are wearing your buoyancy aid and that it is properly secured.

**DO** – sort out the boat and get the sails ready to hoist before you take her to the water. A two-man dinghy will have a jib and a mainsail to get ready, but a single-hander usually has only a mainsail.

**DON'T** – step into the boat until she is afloat. You may put your foot through the bottom.

**DO** – check that the battens in the main-sail are securely fastened in their pockets. Never be tempted to sail without battens. The boat won't sail properly and you may ruin the mainsail.

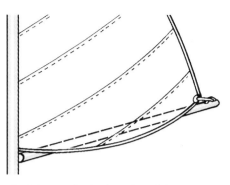

△ A loose-footed mainsail is attached to the end of the boom.

On some single-handed sailing boats such as the *Topper* and the *Laser*, the mainsail has a sleeved luff that slips over the mast before it is stepped into the boat.

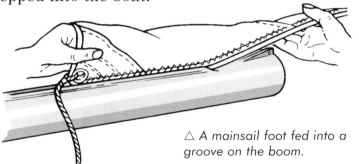

△ A mainsail foot fed into a groove on the boom.

More experienced sailors will hoist their sails while their boat is still ashore. But to start with, you should get everything ready and the boat fully rigged, then hoist the sails when your boat is in the water.

**DO** – get the mainsail ready to hoist. Attach the *halyard* and, with the help of your crew, feed the *luff* of the sail into the groove on the mast. Make sure the main sheet is attached to the boom, and the sail is ready to hoist. In some boats you do not attach the boom to the *gooseneck* until you hoist the sail.

**DO** – get the headsail (jib) ready, if you have one. Secure the *tack* to the bow, secure the luff to the forestay, attach the halyard to the head and lead the sheets correctly down each side of the boat. And **do** get the *luff* really tight when you hoist the sail.

**DO** – learn the right way to secure the halyard after the sail has been hoisted. This is done by securing the halyard to a cleat.

**DO** – check over the whole boat before taking her down to the water.
● Are the bungs in? If they're not your boat will fill with water soon after 'take off'.
● Is the dagger board ready to put in?
● Are there any loose shackles or worn lines?

**DON'T** – allow the rudder blade or dagger board to touch the ground while the boat is in shallow water or it will be damaged.
  Attach the rudder while you are ashore but secure the blade in the lifted position so that it does not drag along the ground when launching.

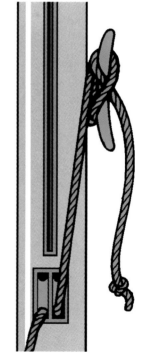

△ Securing a halyard to a mast cleat.

As soon as you get anywhere near your boat or the water start to realise the direction of the wind. Look to see which way the club flag is blowing.

**DON'T** – ever attempt to hoist or lower your sails unless your boat is pointing directly into the wind.

**DON'T** – leave the boat trolley cluttering up the ramp after you have launched the boat. One of the crew should hold the boat while the other one parks the trolley clear of the ramp and above the high water mark. Then whoever is the helmsman gets aboard while the crew continues to hold the boat steady.

If you are single-handed, then you will need someone to help you with the trolley.

**DO** – once you have set off and are in deep enough water, get the rudder fully down, and the dagger board down too. Do this as soon as possible, so that the boat is easier to control.

**DO** – if the wind is blowing towards the shore, have the crew give the boat a good shove away from the shore before they get in. Sometimes it is useful to paddle a little way before you get sailing.

---

### THE WEATHER AND THE TIDE

You will soon realise how important the strength of the wind is to your sailing. To start with, don't worry because your instructor will say if there is too much wind for you. But as soon as you start sailing alone, you will have to judge for yourself. Chapter 7 will tell you a lot about how to understand the weather.

If you are sailing inland, the tide will not worry you, but it will affect you anywhere near the sea. Listen to what the instructor says, use your eyes, and read about the tide in Chapter 10. It is important.

## RETURNING TO THE SHORE

> What you do will depend on the direction of the wind.

### WITH THE WIND BLOWING OFF THE SHORE:
**DO** – be sure to raise your rudder and centreboard before you get into shallow water. You don't want to damage them by hitting the bottom.

**DO** – head the boat into the wind as you reach the shore, the crew can then jump out and hold the bow steady. The helmsman can then lower the mainsail, collect the trolley and prepare to take the boat out of the water.

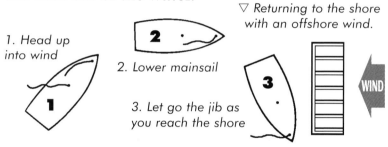

▽ *Returning to the shore with an offshore wind.*

*1. Head up into wind*

*2. Lower mainsail*

*3. Let go the jib as you reach the shore*

WIND

### RETURNING IN AN ONSHORE BREEZE:
**DO** – when the wind is behind you, head up into the wind just before the shallows, and lower the mainsail. Then, with the wind dead behind you, sail in with just the jib which will give you more control. Just as you reach the shore, turn up into the wind so that you are in control and can let go the jib. The crew can then jump out.

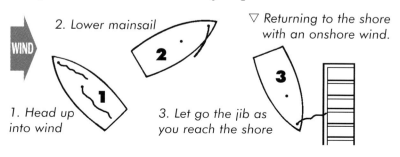

▽ *Returning to the shore with an onshore wind.*

WIND

*2. Lower mainsail*

*1. Head up into wind*

*3. Let go the jib as you reach the shore*

**DON'T** – wherever the boat is – ever try to lower the mainsail unless the boat is pointing into the wind.

**DO** – learn how to take a tow back to shore. There are times when either the wind fails completely or you break something and need a tow from the safety boat.

Usually they will pass you a line. Immediately take a couple of turns around the mast, allowing a long enough end for you to hold on to. This method is secure, but it means that you can let go in an emergency if you need to.

Do not be tempted to secure the tow line to the forestay: it is not strong enough.

▽ To keep the boat balanced during the tow, the crew should sit further aft and the centreboard should be raised halfway. This raises the bow above the water and makes towing more efficient.

---

### GETTING GOING
#### AND COMING BACK TO THE SHORE

These are the two basic but essential drills for using a dinghy. Your instructor may make you practice them several times until you know them really well. Then you can concentrate on enjoying your boat and trying to make it sail fast.

---

**DON'T** – even think of skiving off to the clubhouse or to change until your boat is properly secured and all the gear correctly stowed away.

**DO** – wash down the boat, if water is available, once it is ashore and before you put the cover on.

As well as the hull, wash the blocks and fittings. If you are sailing on the sea, a good wash gets rid of all the salt and the dinghy's gear will last longer.

Sponge out the boat thoroughly, unscrew the hatchcovers and, if possible, let the boat dry out before putting on the cover.

**DO** – tie down the boat cover securely if you are leaving the boat in the dinghy park. In heavy winds you may be advised to tie down the boat itself to prevent it blowing over .

## SAIL CONTROLS – THE SMALL DETAILS

Once you have learned the basic drill of rigging and launching your boat and are starting to sail it, you will find that to make it go really well you need to have your sails trimmed just right.

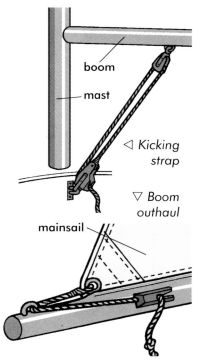

boom

mast

◁ Kicking strap

▽ Boom outhaul

mainsail

The *kicking strap* does an important job. It prevents the boom lifting and going sky high when a strong gust of wind comes along. You will learn to apply a degree of tension to the kicking strap to give the sail the right shape.

The *boom outhaul* is attached to the clew of the mainsail and controls the foot of the sail. As a rough guide it should be tight when beating (see p. 31) and freed off slightly when sailing off the wind.

## Ropes & knots

> There is a lot of rope in any boat, but, just to be difficult, the ropes are always referred to as *lines!*

It is not always easy, but the lines in a boat should be kept tidy. Then you can see what is what, no one trips over them, and they are ready for use when needed.

And if sailors have to handle lines, then they must know how to tie certain knots. Every knot has a special purpose, so learn the right one for the job.

△ **Reef knot** – used for reefing. Not for ropes of unequal size.

△ **Clove hitch** – used for securing a line to a ring or post.

△ **Figure-of-eight knot** – stops rope ends passing through blocks or leads.

△ **Sheet bend** – an ideal knot for securing two ropes of unequal size.

△ **Round turn and two half hitches** – a secure knot for tying to a post or rail.

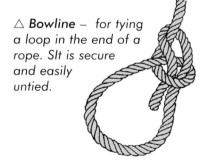

△ **Bowline** – for tying a loop in the end of a rope. SIt is secure and easily untied.

▷ **Rolling hitch** – useful for securing to a post or another rope. Very secure with a lengthwise pull.

CHAPTER 5

# SAFETY

### Playing safe is sensible - not sissy!

We have already talked briefly about safety. To some, always being safe and never taking risks may sound rather dull – perhaps lacking the spirit of adventure, but there is nothing clever about taking *unnecessary* risks.

Which is why when you start sailing you will be required to wear a buoyancy aid or lifejacket, even if you are a good swimmer. And when you start racing you will be disqualified if you do not wear one. You will see that many experienced dinghy sailors continue to wear these even when there is no-one to say that they have to.

If you are taught as a class on the water there will always be a safety boat out with you to help anyone who gets into difficulties. And there is always a safety boat around during races. Again it is a matter of not taking any unnecessary risks.

## LIFEJACKETS AND BUOYANCY AIDS

Although these are both often referred to as 'lifejackets', they are, in fact, different. Dinghy sailors normally wear a buoyancy aid because a proper lifejacket would be too bulky for them to wear in a small boat.

Some lifejackets have a built-in compressed air system that automatically inflates as soon as the wearer enters the water. They are designed to keep the wearer afloat even if they have been knocked unconscious.

### ▷ BUOYANCY AID

*A buoyancy aid is like a padded waistcoat. It is usually fairly lightweight and easy to put on. It will not only help to keep the wearer afloat, but in chilly weather it will help to keep you warm.*

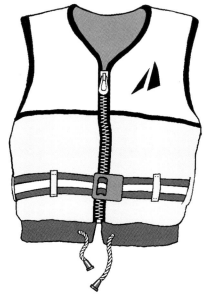

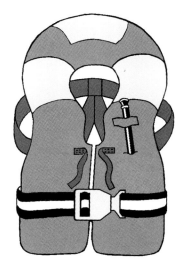

### ◁ LIFEJACKET

*Unlike a buoyancy aid, a lifejacket is inflatable, either by mouth (there is a tube to blow through) or by a small hand-operated gas cylinder. It is designed to keep the wearer's head above water if they are unconscious when they enter the water.*

## IS YOUR BOAT OK?

You must always make sure that your boat is in good shape each time you take it out sailing.

☐ If there is no built-in buoyancy, there will be *buoyancy bags* that must all be fully inflated and well secured so that they will not be washed away if the boat capsizes.

☐ *Paddles* – it's best to carry two.

☐ *Bailer and sponge*. The bailer must be tied to the boat to stop it floating away if you capsize.

## 'STAY WITH THE BOAT'

When you first start to sail, the idea of a capsize may worry you. But you will soon get used to it, and you will be taught how to right a capsized boat. If you have trouble in getting the boat upright again, or even if it is upright but cannot be sailed, never be tempted to swim for the shore.

☐ The golden rule is always: **Stay with the boat**. In addition to your lifejacket, the boat's built-in buoyancy or buoyancy bags will keep you afloat, and you will be far more visible to any rescuer if you are with the boat.

△ Both crew members are wearing buoyancy aids and are taking the sound advice 'Stay with the boat'.

▷ The challenge of ocean racing can be tough going, but both crews and boats are well equipped and prepared for all emergencies.

## WHERE ARE YOU GOING AND WHEN DO YOU PLAN TO BE BACK?

Finally, if you decide to go out sailing on your own, you must tell someone what your plans are. If you plan to go any distance, make sure that someone knows at least in which direction you are going, when you intend to set out, and when you expect to be back.

And then, when you do get back, let them know. Every year a lot of time and money is wasted by the rescue services looking for 'missing' sailors who are, in fact, safely at home but have not bothered to tell anyone of their return.

CHAPTER 6

# THIS IS SAILING

### A simple reminder of how a boat performs with its sails hoisted.

It is obvious that a boat cannot sail directly into the wind. The best she can do is to sail at an angle of about 45° to the wind's direction, although some boats can sail closer than this.

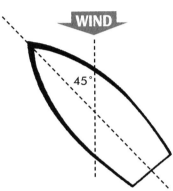

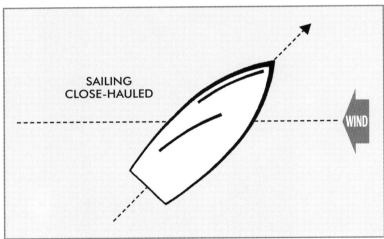

SAILING
CLOSE-HAULED

A boat's sails are controlled by the *sheets*. When she is sailing to windward (sailing towards the direction the wind is coming from, or *on the wind*) the sails are pulled or sheeted in hard almost to the centreline of the boat. With the sails in this position she is sailing *close-hauled*.

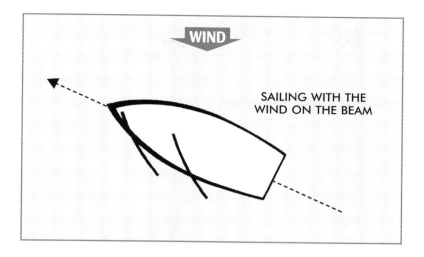

SAILING WITH THE
WIND ON THE BEAM

When you are sailing with the wind on the beam, the boat is said to be *reaching*, which is the fastest and easiest point of sailing. The sheets, which hold in the sails, are eased out.

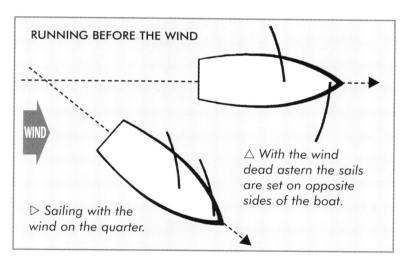

RUNNING BEFORE THE WIND

△ With the wind dead astern the sails are set on opposite sides of the boat.

▷ Sailing with the wind on the quarter.

With the wind *on the quarter* or astern, the sheets are eased even more and the boat is said to be *running*. You must take care when running as a freak gust of wind can make the boom swing over to the other side of the boat and give you a nasty bang on the head if you are not prepared for it.

## STEERING TO WINDWARD

Being able to sail a boat well to windward is an important skill for the helmsman, because the closer you can *point* the boat towards the wind, the more quickly you can sail towards a windward destination. It is a matter of heading as close to the wind as possible, while keeping the boat sailing fast.

If you point the boat too close to the wind (pointing 'too high'), you will be told you are *pinching* and the boat will not sail properly. Practice and concentration are needed!

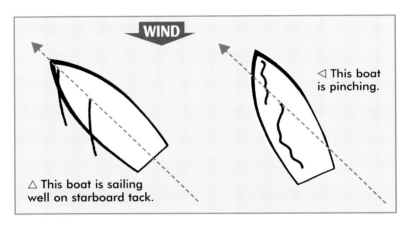

WIND

◁ This boat is pinching.

△ This boat is sailing well on starboard tack.

## SAILING TO WINDWARD

Because she cannot sail directly into the wind, a boat making for a destination that is upwind has to steer a zigzag course. This is called *beating*.

Tacking is the process of altering course with the wind ahead until the sails are set on the other side. The boat is then on a new tack.

A boat on *starboard tack* has the wind coming from her starboard side and her boom on the port side. A boat on *port tack* has the wind coming from her port side and the boom on the starboard side.

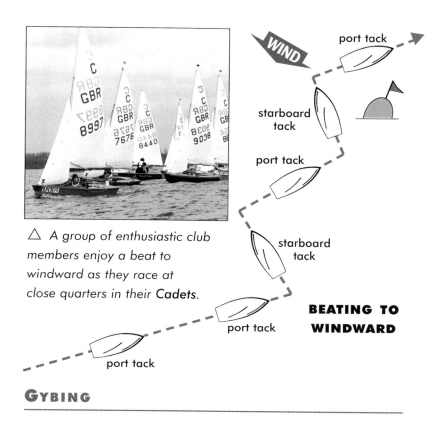

△ A group of enthusiastic club members enjoy a beat to windward as they race at close quarters in their **Cadets**.

## GYBING

This is the opposite to tacking. The boat's course is altered so that the wind passes across the stern and the sails are then set on the other side.

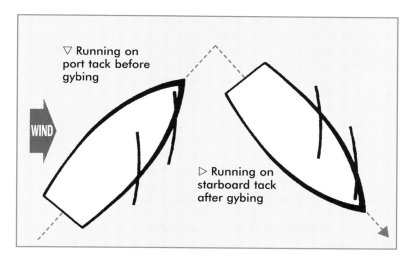

CHAPTER 7

# THE WEATHER

Like any sailor you will enjoy yourself more when you are sailing on a fine sunny day. But you will soon find that, regardless of the weather, the strength of the wind is what really matters. The sun may shine, but it will be no fun in a flat calm with not enough wind to sail. However – especially in the early days – you do not want so much wind that you cannot handle your boat easily. So you need a 'nice sailing breeze'.

◁ The sea is calm and there is not enough wind for sailing.

◁ A good sailing breeze makes for pleasant sailing.

◁ The strong wind has made the sea rough and it is far too strong for safe dinghy sailing.

To start with, you will not have to worry because your instructor will tell you if there is too much wind for you to go sailing.

However, all sailors ought to be 'weather wise'. This means trying to find out in advance what the weather is *going* to do, but always keeping an eye open for what it is *actually* doing.

☐   When you start going out alone, it will be up to you to make sure that the weather is OK for your amount of experience. This means not only being aware of what the weather is like when you set out, but what it may be like in a couple of hour's time.

---

### BEWARE SUNBURN!

Because the sun reflects off the water you **will** get sunburnt if you don't protect yourself. Always apply plenty of high factor, water-resistant protection cream whenever you go afloat. Ultra violet rays can also penetrate clouds.

---

**WEATHER FORECASTS –**
**YOU SHOULD KNOW HOW TO GET ONE**

In most clubs the weather forecast is posted up each day. If this is not the case and you specially need one, you will find that there is a local Met Office telephone number which you can call for a forecast. Some local BBC radio stations also broadcast coastal weather forecasts. In any case, if you do need a weather forecast ask someone where you can get one.

It is also interesting to look at the TV weather forecast. Of course, it covers the whole country and cannot give the particular details for your area, but it will give you a useful general picture of what the weather may be like.

## SOMETHING YOU SHOULD KNOW

## The Beaufort Scale

- In weather forecasts you will hear references to 'South Easterly force 3' (or, on a bad day it might even be 'gale force 8'!) so you must know what this means.

- The Beaufort Scale is used to measure wind speed. It was devised back in 1806 by a British Admiral, Sir Francis Beaufort, and for a long time it has been used throughout the world.

- Wind speeds are measured in knots, and a knot is a nautical mile per hour.

| Force | Speed (Knots) | Description |
|---|---|---|
| 0 | 0 – 1 | Calm |
| 1 | 1 – 3 | Light air |
| 2 | 4 – 6 | Light breeze |
| 3 | 7 – 10 | Gentle breeze |
| 4 | 11 – 16 | Moderate breeze |
| 5 | 17 – 21 | Fresh breeze |
| 6 | 22 – 27 | Strong breeze |
| 7 | 28 – 33 | Near gale |
| 8 | 34 – 40 | Gale |
| 9 | 41 – 47 | Severe gale |
| 10 | 48 – 55 | Storm |
| 11 | 56 – 63 | Violent strom |
| 12 | 64 plus | Hurricane |

The descriptions can be misleading. We may think of a breeze as something gentle, but force 5 – which is described as a 'fresh breeze' – is a far stronger wind than you will want for sailing a small boat.

## WATCH OUT FOR THE OFFSHORE WIND

An offshore wind means that it is blowing from the shore towards the water. That is, it is behind you if you stand on the shore and look out across the water.

An offshore wind can be deceptive. It may not feel very strong because of the shelter of the land, and the water near to the shore will be calm.

But once you get afloat and the offshore wind carries you nicely away from the shore, you may find that it is stronger than you thought. It is then that you will discover how difficult it is to get back to the shore again.

▷ Windsurfers in particular should pay attention to the direction of the wind. They can easily get into trouble from an offshore wind if they cannot manage to sail back inshore again.

### SAFETY TIP

When you are sailing the wind can also feel lighter when you are running with it behind you. Take care when running before an offshore breeze, because when you turn into the wind to head for home, it will be much stronger than you expect.

CHAPTER 8

# THIS IS RACING

Why race? Because it is the best way to improve your sailing skills. And racing is fun!

## WHAT IS A DINGHY RACE?

Quite simply, a dinghy race is where a fleet of dinghies set off from a starting line, and sail round a course marked with buoys.

*Fleet racing* is where all the boats in the race are identical. The winner is the first boat to cross the line.

*Handicap racing* is where a number of dinghies of different classes race together. A handicap system is used to work out the winner.

> Essentially races are won by good sailors sailing good boats, and a shiny new dinghy will not win if it is badly sailed. But a good sailor can do well, even in a modest boat.

### THE COURSE

The course is round a number of buoys (referred to as *marks*), laid by the club, with letters or numbers on them, and which have to be rounded in a certain order. In an estuary, navigation buoys can be used as part of the course.

*The Race Officer* – the person who is organising the racing for the day – will set a course depending on the wind direction. This is almost always planned so that the first leg of the course after the start is a beat to windward. He will also decide how many times round the course you will sail before the finish.

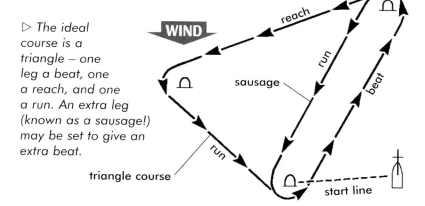

▷ *The ideal course is a triangle – one leg a beat, one a reach, and one a run. An extra leg (known as a sausage!) may be set to give an extra beat.*

There may be a pre-race briefing, when the course is fully explained. Usually you will be shown a plan of the course, or just the numbers of the buoys to be rounded, and the number of rounds to be sailed. Look out across the water from the shore and try to spot the marks.

### THE STARTLINE

Many clubs have a *race box* (a hut) with a flagstaff on it, and another flagstaff or pole in front of it. The start line is formed by these two in line (*in transit*). A buoy will mark the outer end of the line. This is called a *fixed line start*.

The club may also use a *committee boat* at one end of the start line; it is usually a power boat fitted with a flagstaff and boards for showing course details. The start line is an imaginary line from the committee boat's flagstaff to a buoy at the other end of the line.

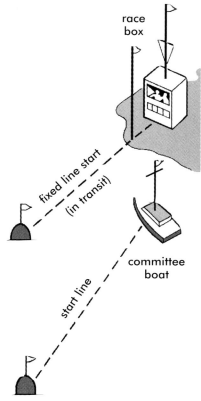

Start lines may vary, but they are quite easy to understand. Before your first race, or if you are racing at a new club, walk along and look at the start line before you go afloat.

### STARTING SIGNALS

☐ Starting signals are often referred to as *guns* even though a horn or whistle, and not a gun, may be used. However, guns are used for major events.

Remember that sound signals are there to attract your attention to the flags. It is the flags, not the guns, that tell you what to do.

☐ There is a class flag for each class of boat that is racing. You must know the flag for your class.

☐ The count down sequence for the start of a race used to be signals at ten minutes before the start and then at five minutes. But nowadays, some clubs are using six minutes and three minutes, or even four and two. It makes things move more quickly – there may be shorter races but more of them.

So this is how it goes:

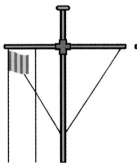 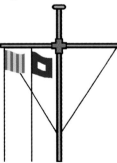 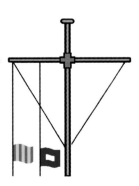

*10 – 6 minutes before start*
(10 minute gun)
The class flag is hoisted.

*5 – 3 minutes to go*
(5 minute gun)
Preparatory signal
Internaional Code
flag **P** (Blue Peter).

*The start*
Both the flags, the class flag and the Code flag **P**, are lowered.

## AT THE START

When the gun goes your boat must be completely on the pre-start side of the line.

If the Race Officer sees any part of any boat over the line at the start signal, he will hoist flag X (blue cross on white) and make a second sound signal. It's up to you to recognize that you are the boat (or one of the boats) over the line at the start. If so, you must turn round to make a new start (keeping clear of the boats that are racing).

If the Race Officer sees that the majority of the fleet was over the line at the start, he may recall the whole fleet by making two sound signals and hoisting the first substitute flag (blue and yellow triangle).

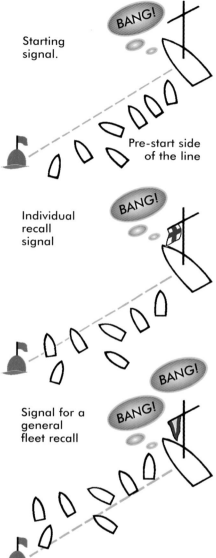

Starting signal.

Pre-start side of the line

Individual recall signal

Signal for a general fleet recall

---

### SO THIS IS WHAT YOU MUST KNOW
### BEFORE THE RACE

1. The course. Be absolutely clear – which direction? Which marks? You can write it all down.
2. Your class flag. What does it look like?
3. The timing. Are the signals going to be 10 mins then 5, 6 then 3, or what?

## THE RACING RULES...

You will find simple explanations of the most important rules in the next chapter. If you are going to race, you must read them.

### SAILING THE RACE - Some expert tips

**AT THE START** – Start your watch at the first gun, and keep an eye on the time. Check it at the second gun.
  *You will need a simple timer or stopwatch for racing. Practice reading your watch as well as keeping an eye on your sailing.*
  Aim to have your sails trimmed and be sailing at full speed towards the first mark so that you cross the line immediately after the starting signal – but not a moment before. This needs practice! The port and starboard rule (see opposite above) is especially important when manoeuvring before the start.

**THE BEAT** – The first leg of the race is almost always a beat to windward.

• Sheet in the sails and keep the boat moving through the water all the time.

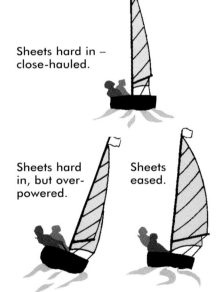

Sheets hard in – close-hauled.

• Keep the boat flat by sitting out as hard as you can. Remember – a flat boat is a fast boat.

• If the wind is overpowering you, even when you and your crew are both sitting out hard, free off the mainsail a little to depower the boat – this is called spilling the wind. As soon as the gust passes, sheet in again to keep the power on.

Sheets hard in, but over-powered.

Sheets eased.

• When you start racing, it is very easy to get engrossed with your own sailing and forget about the other boats around you. Always look out for other boats, particularly if you are on port tack, when you are the give-way boat. When you are on starboard tack you can warn port tack boats that you are there by shouting *'Starboard!'*.

## ...AND A REMINDER!

The single most important rule is that a boat on the starboard tack has right of way over a boat on the port tack. *The port tack boat must give way.*

**MARK ROUNDING** – When you reach the first mark, round it with plenty of room to avoid hitting it. As you round the mark, don't forget to free off the mainsheet and jib as you go. Lift the centreboard slightly and balance the boat to keep it flat.

Leave plenty of room when you round a mark.

**OFFWIND LEGS** – Once you have rounded the first windward mark, look out for the next mark and check the wind direction. If you are on a reach, aim the boat at the next mark and ease the mainsheet and jib slightly to keep the boat flat.

Ease the sails as you head for the next mark.

• When you get more experienced at racing, trimming sails on a reach is vital to ensure that you get every little bit of speed from your boat. While the helmsman sheets the main in and out in the gusts and lulls, the crew concentrates on doing the same with the jib.

Sails eased out on a comfortable run.

**RUNNING** – If you find yourself on a run with the wind behind you, keep an eye on the burgee to make sure that you aren't running *by the lee* (which means with the wind on the wrong side of the mainsail). In this situation, the crew can keep one hand on the boom to prevent an unexpected gybe.

Keep an eye on the boom when running with the wind right aft in case the boom slams over.

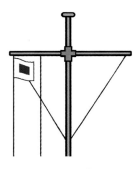

## SHORTENING COURSE

Sometimes, if the wind drops, the Race Officer may well decide to shorten the course. He will do this by making two sound signals and hoisting Code flag **S**.

## THE FINISH LINE

Once you have crossed the finish line, sail away from it, and don't obstruct other boats still racing.

## BACK ON SHORE

Check to see if you have to sign off after the race. Some clubs insist on this, and failure to do so might mean you are disqualified.

## PENALTIES

In your first couple of races it is worthwhile trying to keep out of trouble as much as you can, although sometimes it is unavoidable. But there are a couple of ways to excuse yourself.

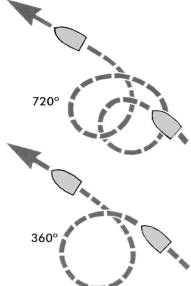

If you break the rule in a port/starboard situation, you may excuse yourself by sailing well clear of other boats and doing a 720 degree turn. This includes bearing away, gybing, tacking, gybing and tacking, all in quick succession.

If you break the rules by touching a mark, you may excuse yourself by making a 360 degree turn (one gybe and one tack).

# CHAPTER 9

# THE RACING RULES

**Rules can be a bore, but all sports need rules in order to work. Top level dinghy racing is very competitive, so very exact rules are necessary.**

The real purpose of the racing rules is to prevent boats bumping into each other. The main question is, which boat should get out of the way of the other – after all, you are in a dinghy, not a dodgem car.

The complete set of racing rules is quite long and complicated – so that's the bad news. The good news is that there are only about half a dozen really important rules which you need to know to get started. And once you have learned these (which you must do) the others will follow easily.

Before you start to learn these basic rules, you must understand a handful of simple terms, some of which you will have come across already (see Chapter 6). Not only are they used in the racing rules, but they are a basic part of sailing.

△ *These single-sail Lasers battle against a brisk breeze as they race towards the windward mark.*

## PORT TACK AND STARBOARD TACK

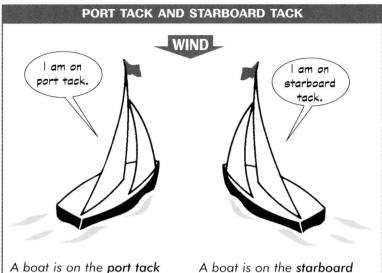

A boat is on the **port tack** when the wind is coming from the port side and the boom is on the starboard side.

A boat is on the **starboard tack** when the wind is coming from the starboard side and the boom is on the port side.

## CLOSE HAULED AND FREE

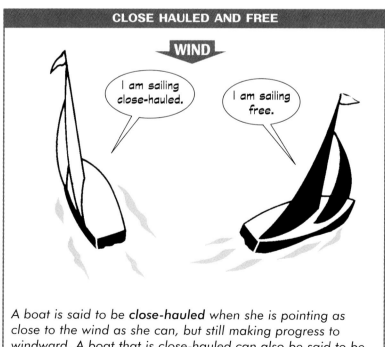

A boat is said to be **close-hauled** when she is pointing as close to the wind as she can, but still making progress to windward. A boat that is close-hauled can also be said to be 'on the wind'. She is **sailing free** when she is not close hauled.

## WINDWARD AND LEEWARD

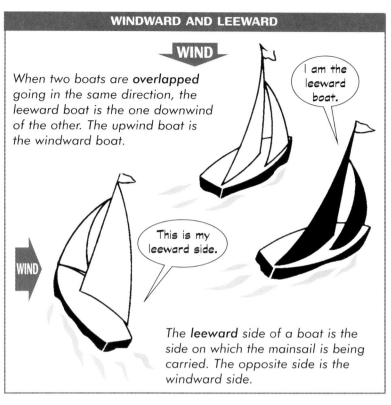

When two boats are **overlapped** going in the same direction, the leeward boat is the one downwind of the other. The upwind boat is the windward boat.

*I am the leeward boat.*

*This is my leeward side.*

The **leeward** side of a boat is the side on which the mainsail is being carried. The opposite side is the windward side.

## LUFFING

*Look out! He's going to luff!*

*Yes, and I have right of way!*

A boat is **luffing** when she alters course towards the direction of the wind. For instance, apart from racing, a boat may luff up to lower her sails.

## BEARING AWAY

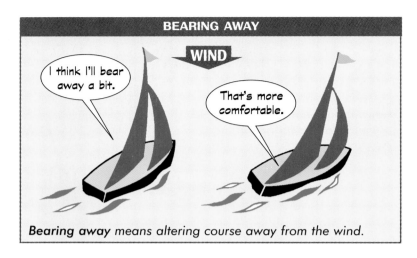

*Bearing away* means altering course away from the wind.

## TACKING AND GYBING

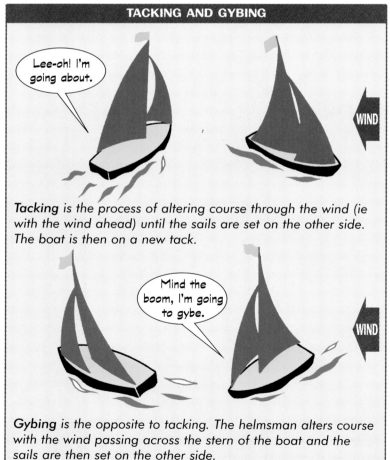

*Tacking* is the process of altering course through the wind (ie with the wind ahead) until the sails are set on the other side. The boat is then on a new tack.

*Gybing* is the opposite to tacking. The helmsman alters course with the wind passing across the stern of the boat and the sails are then set on the other side.

## CLEAR AHEAD, CLEAR ASTERN AND OVERLAPPED

These are essentially racing terms and they may sound difficult to understand. Look at the drawings and they will become clear.

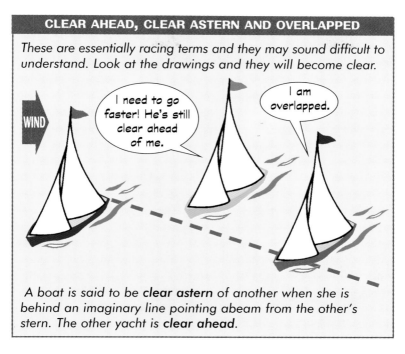

A boat is said to be **clear astern** of another when she is behind an imaginary line pointing abeam from the other's stern. The other yacht is **clear ahead**.

## WINDWARD MARK AND LEEWARD MARK

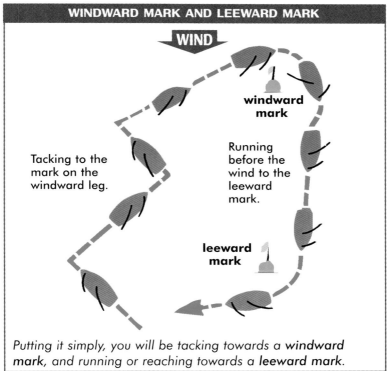

Putting it simply, you will be tacking towards a **windward mark**, and running or reaching towards a **leeward mark**.

# THE RACING RULES THAT YOU *MUST* KNOW

## BASIC RIGHT-OF-WAY IN OPEN WATER

**WHEN BOTH BOATS ARE IN OPEN WATER AND NOT ABOUT TO ROUND A MARK**

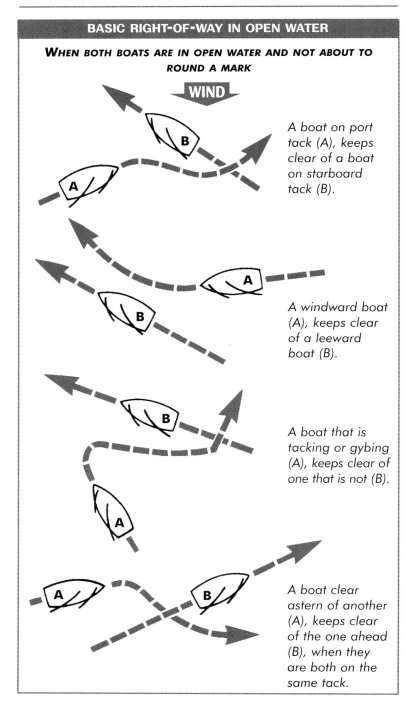

**WIND**

A boat on port tack (A), keeps clear of a boat on starboard tack (B).

A windward boat (A), keeps clear of a leeward boat (B).

A boat that is tacking or gybing (A), keeps clear of one that is not (B).

A boat clear astern of another (A), keeps clear of the one ahead (B), when they are both on the same tack.

## BASIC RIGHT-OF-WAY AT AN OFFWIND MARK

### *The mark you have sailed to on a reach or a run*

**1.** Having gained an overlap within two boat lengths of the mark, the boat on the inside must be given room to round it. The port and starboard rule does not apply in this instance.

**2.** A boat that reaches the mark clear ahead of another has the right to round the mark, and the other boat must keep clear.

**3.** The inside boat must make a proper job of rounding the mark so that she keeps clear of the boat that is giving her room.

## BASIC RIGHT-OF-WAY AT A WINDWARD MARK

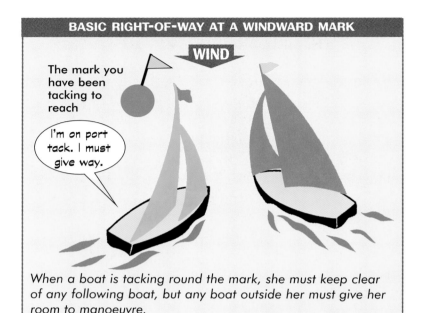

When a boat is tacking round the mark, she must keep clear of any following boat, but any boat outside her must give her room to manoeuvre.

## CHANGING COURSE

Whenever a boat with right of way changes course, she must allow the boat that gives way enough room to keep clear.

## BASIC RIGHTS BEFORE AND AT THE START

The racing rules usually apply from 5 minutes before the start

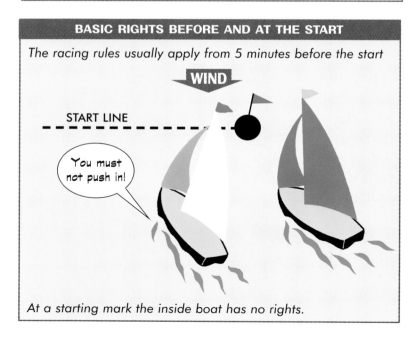

At a starting mark the inside boat has no rights.

## WHEN BOATS ARE *NOT* RACING – 'THE RULE OF THE ROAD'

The racing rules above apply between boats that are racing together. But, in fact, most ships and boats on the water are *not* racing. So there also has to be a sort of marine Highway Code (known as **The Rule of the Road**) to prevent collisions.

For the moment there is not much here that need worry you, but there are a few things you should know:

☐  If you are out sailing but not racing, keep well away from boats that are racing. This is not in any rules – it's common sense and good manners – and will save you being sworn at!

☐  When two sailing boats meet, port still gives way to starboard, whether you are racing or not. **The Rule of the Road** says so.

☐  But if you are overtaking another boat when you are not racing, *you* must keep clear.

☐ By the rules, power gives way to sail, which means that motor boats should keep clear of sailing boats. When there are a lot of sails on the water, motor boats should try to keep well away from them.

☐ But in a narrow channel – which means the approach to any port or harbour – yachts and dinghies must keep clear of any merchant ships. The bigger ships will have to stay in the deeper water of the channel and may not have enough room or time to get out of the way.

This means keeping well clear. Just missing is not clever or funny!

☐ You must also realise that large ships take a long time to alter course in order to avoid another vessel. Make a bold alteration to your course and do it in plenty of time so that they can see what you are doing. Collisions usually happen when one boat (or ship) does not understand what the other is doing.

CHAPTER 10

# UNDERSTANDING THE TIDE

If you are sailing on a lake or a reservoir, there will be no tide to worry about. But you will soon find that anywhere near the sea, such as in a harbour or an estuary, the tide can have quite an effect on your sailing. You need to understand how and why this happens.

You can see the tide move in two ways:

☐ Firstly, it rises and falls. Note that sailors mostly talk about **high water** and **low water** rather than high and low tide – although it is not really important.

☐ Then there is the horizontal movement of the tide – the **tidal stream**. This is the tide **flooding** up an estuary (when it's coming in) and then **ebbing** out to sea again (when it's going out).

## LET'S LOOK AT THE RISE AND FALL FIRST

It may be easier to launch your boat at high water than when the tide is low, but more importantly, when you are sailing you will find shallow patches which you can cross quite happily at high water and where you will get stuck on the bottom at low water.

So the depth of water anywhere depends on the height of the tide. This may not matter so much where the water is deep, but closer inshore, the height of the tide becomes very important.

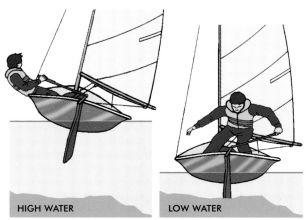

▷ Crossing a sandbank at high water can be safe. At low water you could run aground if you have not studied your tide tables.

HIGH WATER       LOW WATER

## SPRING TIDES AND NEAP TIDES

There is no room here for a full explanation of these terms, but let's just say that the movement of the tide is controlled by the moon's position in relation to the sun.

So when the moon is new, and when it is full (or a couple of days later to be precise), we have *spring tides* when the tidal *range* is at its greatest, which means that the high water is highest during the month, and the low water lowest.

Half way between the new moon and the full moon we have *neap tides* when the tidal range is

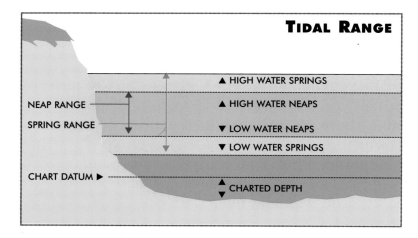

TIDAL RANGE

NEAP RANGE

SPRING RANGE

▲ HIGH WATER SPRINGS

▲ HIGH WATER NEAPS

▼ LOW WATER NEAPS

▼ LOW WATER SPRINGS

CHART DATUM ▶

CHARTED DEPTH

least, so that there will not be such a large rise and fall between high water and low water. Dates of spring and neap tides are shown in tide tables.

## THE TIDAL STREAM

If the level of water in a harbour is going to rise, then clearly water has to flow in from the sea. When the tide is falling it will flow out again.

When you are out on the water you will soon notice this *tidal stream* flowing in and out of a harbour or estuary. Trying to sail against the stream is quite different from sailing happily along with it. If you are sailing or rowing across the direction of the tidal stream you notice it even more, as you get pushed sideways in the direction of the flow.

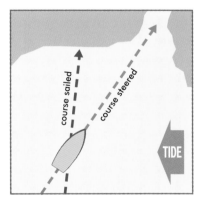

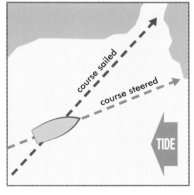

△ This boat has steered for the harbour entrance and the tide has pushed it off course.

△ This boat has steered to compensate for the tide and has arrived where it wants to be.

In general the tide floods from the time of low water until high water is reached. Then it ebbs until it is low water again. At both high and low water, the tide doesn't immediately put on the brakes and change direction.There is a period called *slack water* when the tide hardly moves in either direction before it changes again.

---

### BE TIDEWISE

When you go sailing always try to know roughly the times of high water and low water, and what the tidal range (the amount of its rise and fall) is. Then you will know what the tidal stream is doing. Not a big deal, but it will help you to sail your boat better and more successfully. And it can be very important when you are racing.

---

## MAKING THE BEST USE OF THE TIDE

In a river or estuary the stream does not flow at the same speed everywhere. It tends to flow more strongly in the middle of a channel, and be weaker nearer the shore. It may also change direction closer in towards the side of a channel before it does in the middle of the channel.

This is particularly important when you are racing.

☐ Obviously if you are trying to sail *against* the stream (ie you have a *foul tide*), you need to be sailing where the tide is weakest.

☐ If you are sailing *with* the stream (when the tide is said to be *fair*), you clearly want to be where it is strongest.

But above all, to tell the tide's direction, watch other boats at anchor or swinging on moorings.

▽ *You can get a good idea of the strength and direction of the tide by watching it swish against a buoy.*

Slack water          Tide running

## SPOTTING HOW THE TIDE IS RUNNING

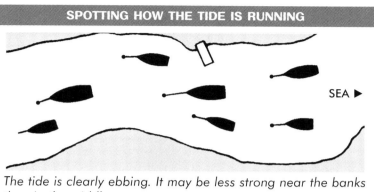

The tide is clearly ebbing. It may be less strong near the banks than in the middle.

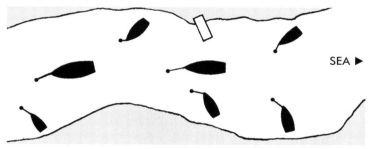

It is getting near the turn of the tide. The tide is slack near the banks, and may be starting to turn there.

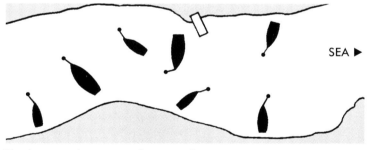

Slack water. It may not last very long.

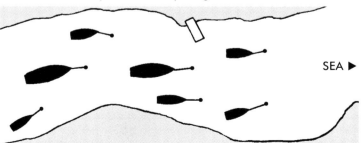

The flood tide has started.

CHAPTER 11

# CHARTS

### The sailor's road maps.

You will not normally use a chart in a dinghy, but they are always interesting to study. Looking at your local chart is the best way to get to know your regular sailing waters, or to investigate a new sailing area. Most sailing clubs have a local chart posted up in their clubhouse.

There are charts which cover whole oceans, charts which cover specific stretches of coastline, and harbour plans, which show important local details. The chart on the page opposite shows the entrance to Salcombe Harbour in South Devon.

*Soundings* (the depth of the water) are shown in metres; a figure such as $3_2$ means 3.2 metres. But on old charts soundings are given in *fathoms*; a fathom is six feet.

Charts not only show features at sea (on the water areas) but also relevant points to note on the land, such as conspicuous buildings like churches etc.

Sailors not only need to know where they are, but what the depth of water is. This is not so important in a dinghy, but vital for a large vessel whose hull may be several metres below the water. So the figures scattered around on the water areas of the chart are *soundings* giving the depth of water in that spot.

## SCALE AND DISTANCE

Although metres are used for measuring depth, kilometres are not used at sea. The unit of distance

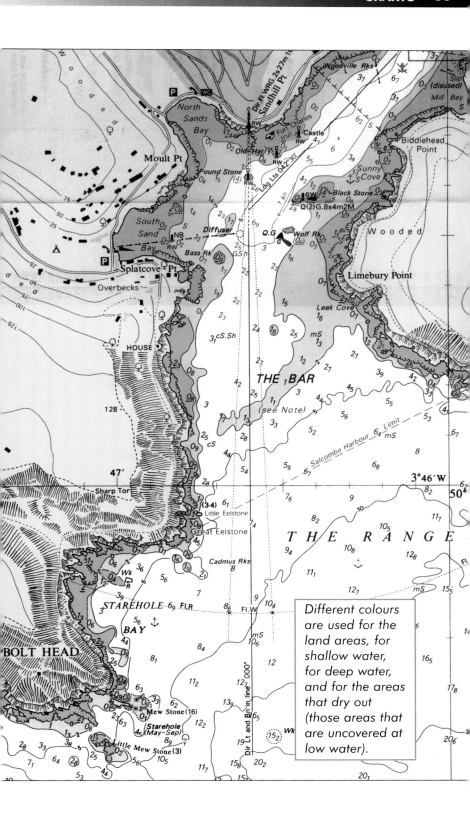

Different colours are used for the land areas, for shallow water, for deep water, and for the areas that dry out (those areas that are uncovered at low water).

used at sea is a *nautical mile* which is 2,000 yards (or a minute of latitude). Local charts usually have a distance scale like a road map.

Note that a chart shows the least depth of water to be expected anywhere. (And if you remember what you read about tides in the last chapter, this will be at low water springs.)

So the area of water to the East of Salcombe town is shown in green, which means that it *dries out* and is visible at low water. But this still means that for much of the time it is covered by water, although it is very shallow.

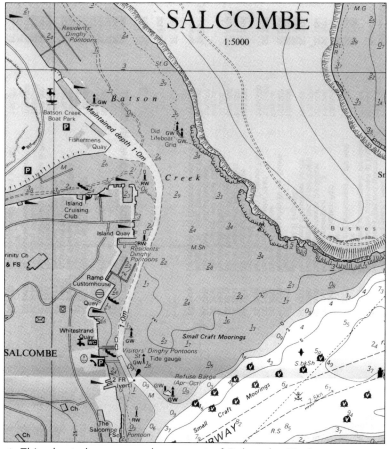

△ This chart shows an enlargement of Salcombe Harbour, an area where there is a lot of dinghy sailing.

## LIGHTS

As you will probably do most of your sailing in daylight, you need not be much concerned with lighthouses and buoys with coloured lights, but looking out over the water at night you may see them flashing, and may like to know what the flashes mean.

If a sailor out at sea sights a lighthouse flashing, he must be able to know which lighthouse it is. And in a channel marked by lit buoys, he must be able to know which buoy is which. So all these lights have a different pattern of flashes, and sometimes the light has a different colour.

Look at the chart and you will see that lighthouses and lit buoys have a purple blip alongside them, with a code showing the pattern of its flashes – this is called the light's *characteristic*.

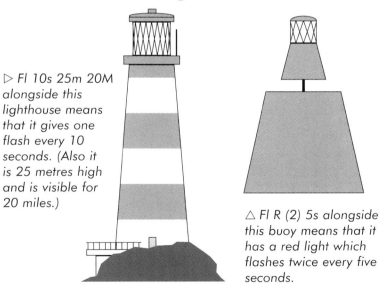

▷ Fl 10s 25m 20M alongside this lighthouse means that it gives one flash every 10 seconds. (Also it is 25 metres high and is visible for 20 miles.)

△ Fl R (2) 5s alongside this buoy means that it has a red light which flashes twice every five seconds.

If you see a lit buoy or a lighthouse at night, count the flashes and work out its characteristic. It's good practice for when you really need to know!

CHAPTER 12

# BUOYS

**When you sail past a navigation buoy in an estuary or in the approaches to a harbour, you need to understand why it is there.**

Navigation buoys have two jobs – either to guide or to warn sailors.

They guide sailors by marking the edges of deep water channels, and they warn them against dangers such as rocks and sandbanks.

Their purpose is shown by their colour and shape, and sometimes by a topmark. They all have a name or a number painted on them. Some buoys have a distinguishing light on top that allows them to be identified at night. Their size varies from the big buoys used in the approach channel to a major port, to quite small unlit buoys marking a creek.

| LATERAL BUOYS | SAFE WATER MARKS |
|---|---|
| 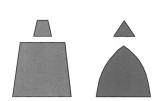 |   |
| These buoys mark the sides of a channel. On the starboard side (coming in from the sea) the buoys are green and conical shaped. On the port side they are red and can shaped. | These buoys have red and white vertical stripes. Usually placed at the approach to a channel and varying in shape, they mark the entrance to the channel – there is safe water all round them. |

## CARDINAL BUOYS

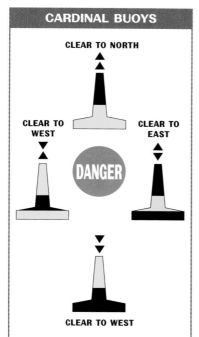

CLEAR TO NORTH

CLEAR TO WEST

CLEAR TO EAST

DANGER

CLEAR TO WEST

These buoys are called Cardinal buoys because they are sited North, South, East and West of a particular danger; and N,S,E and W are the cardinal points of the compass. They are yellow and black in different combinations, and the topmark on each buoy is different.

## ISOLATED DANGER MARKS

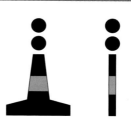

*You may not see many of these, but you should learn to recognise them. They mark an isolated danger, and there is clear water all round them. However, it is wise not to approach them too closely.*

### REMEMBER!

Never tie your boat up to any navigation buoy (unless you have a *serious* problem). It is the wrong thing to do, and you could actually end up in trouble from the Harbourmaster.

## SPECIAL MARKS

*These buoys are yellow and they may be any shape – conical, round, can or beacon. Sometimes they have an X topmark. They are not navigation marks, but mark specific features such as a fish farm.*

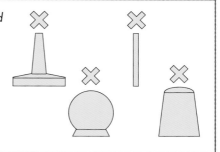

CHAPTER 13

# EXPLORING IN A DINGHY

**Racing is fun, but when you can handle your boat well, you may want a change of pace and do some exploring instead.**

A dinghy is ideal for exploring creeks and estuaries. It has a shallow draft and can be made shallower still by lifting your centreboard. So you can visit areas where larger, deep-keeled boats cannot go.

You can, of course, explore in a small single-handed dinghy, *but if you go on your own, remember to tell someone where you are going.* However, it is usually better to go in a larger dinghy because you can take things for a picnic ashore or even a tent and sleeping bags for camping. Sometimes an expedition can be organised with two or three boats.

Sailing further afield is also a good opportunity to put into practice what you have learned about charts and about the tide. Charts are far too expensive to get wet and damaged in a small boat. So study your chart before you set out to get a good idea of where you are going. Then, if you take your chart afloat, make sure you have it well protected in a clear, waterproof plastic bag.

Work out the times of high and low water for the day you plan to go exploring. Is it springs or neaps? Or is it somewhere in between? It may, for instance, be a good idea to have an easy sail up river with the flood tide helping you along, and then come back down again on the ebb tide.

You may decide to plan a visit ashore. If so, where will you park your boat? Will you be able to haul it up a beach? A sandy beach can be fine, but mud can be a disaster – even dangerous in places.

You should know what the tide is doing, but if you don't, a further useful guide is: a wet beach means that the tide is falling, and a dry beach means a rising tide.

If the tide is rising and you are going to leave your boat for a while, then you clearly must carry it above the high water mark. If, for instance, you are going to spend the night camping ashore, you must be absolutely certain that your boat will be quite safe during the night.

Generally, a boat should be carried up a beach, as it may get damaged if it is dragged. Of course, if the tide is falling fast, you won't want to carry it too far or it will mean a long haul back to get it in the water again. It's not really very complicated but organising your plans around what the tide is doing, and what it is going to do, is certainly worth a bit of thought.

△ Always carry your dinghy from the water. If you drag it ashore you will damage the hull on the stones and gravel on the shore.

When you are exploring away from your home base, there may not be many chances to tie up alongside a dock or jetty. But if you happen to find a place where you think you can go alongside, there are three important things to remember.

**1.** Are you allowed to go alongside? Is it a public jetty or is it private? Look around for someone to ask. If it is a jetty belonging to another club, ask someone in the clubhouse if you can use it.

**2.** Unless the jetty has its own fenders, you must put out your own fenders to prevent your boat being damaged. This applies to any boat of any size anywhere.

**3.** Then you have to think about the tide again.

△ Fenders out for safety.

△ You don't want this to happen!

△ Dinghy club members tidying up their boats and coming ashore for a night's camping after a day exploring a shallow river.

# CHAPTER 14

# DINGHY SPOTTING

There are more than a hundred different dinghy classes in the UK alone, and so that they can be recognised, every class has its own logo which is shown on the sail.

Here are some that you are likely to see out sailing.

**Albacore** – two-man 15ft racing dinghy.

**Boss** – fast, twin-trapeze racing boat with spinnaker.

**Bosun** – strong, safe, developed by the Royal Navy for training.

**Buzz** – high performance with a spinnaker and single trapeze.

**Cadet** – popular racing dinghy for under 18 year olds.

**Comet** – three models, one with a mainsail only.

**Enterprise** – simple, and very popular for training and racing.

**Finn** – Fast, Olympic class singlehander.

**Fireball** – international class with spinnaker and trapeze.

**Firefly** – two-man, glassfibre or wooden one-design. Popular for team racing.

**420** – *two-man one-design, popular for youth training.*

 **505** – *international high-performance racer with spinnaker and single trapeze.*

 **Flying Fifteen** – *fast, two-man 20ft keelboat with spinnaker.*

 **GP Fourteen** – *general purpose two-man dinghy with spinnaker.*

 **Graduate** – *simple dinghy, with no trapeze and no spinnaker.*

 **Gull** – *glassfibre/wood, racing and family boat.*

 **Heron** – *simple family boat with spinnaker.*

 **Hobie Cat** – *a range of different sized multihulls.*

 **Hornet** – *hard-chine racer with trapeze and spinnaker.*

 **International 14** – *hi-tec, high performance development class.*

 **Javelin** –*two-man racer with spinnaker and trapeze.*

 **Kestrel** –*16ft glassfibre racing boat with spinnaker.*

 **Lark** – *one-design with spinnaker. Popular for team racing.*

 **Laser** – *many types and sizes with this basic logo.*

 **Merlin Rocket** – *long established, broad beam racer with spinnaker.*

**Miracle** –wood/glassfibre simple family boat.

**Mirror** – popular one-design, suitable for home construction.

**National Twelve** – highly developed, two-man racing dinghy.

**OK** – single-handed racer.

**Optimist** – small racing dinghy ideally suited to the under 18s.

**Osprey** – racing dinghy with spinnaker and trapeze.

**RS** – several boats. RS200 very popular with beginners.

**Scorpion** – two-man racing dinghy with spinnaker.

**Signet** – 12ft all-purpose dinghy.

**Snipe** – internationally  popular racing dinghy. (No trapeze or spinnaker.)

**Solo** – single-hander, with fully-battened mainsail.

**Streaker** – light, fast, single-hander.

**Topper** – highly popular single-hander.

**Wanderer** – strong and roomy, all-purpose dinghy. Good for beginners.

**Wayfarer** – classic all-round family racing boat.

CHAPTER 15

# SAILING IN BIGGER BOATS

**A boat becomes a yacht when it is big enough for her crew to live aboard.**

Once you've become a competent dinghy sailor you may get invited to sail in a larger sailing yacht.

If you are keen to sail on a larger yacht, ask around at your club to see if anyone needs an extra crew. Or perhaps a friend's father owns a yacht and needs an extra hand.

As far as sailing the boat is concerned there is no real difference between a yacht and a dinghy. There are still halyards and sheets, and you will still be tacking and gybing. It is just a matter of size.

However, there is one important difference; even in relatively light weather, the pull on a yacht's sheet will be much stronger than you expect and you will have to learn to handle them correctly.

## WORKING THE BOAT

When you are part of a yacht's crew, you will have to do more than just sail the boat. Many yachts are berthed in a marina and when the yacht departs for its cruise, the whole crew has to help with the lines and fend-

▷ *A cruising yacht anchored for the night.*

ers, and then stow them away. And later, when she returns to her berth, there will be plenty for the crew to do securing the lines ashore.

Another difference is that many yachts anchor for the night when they are away cruising. The crew must learn how to let go the anchor correctly – and how to haul it up again the next morning.

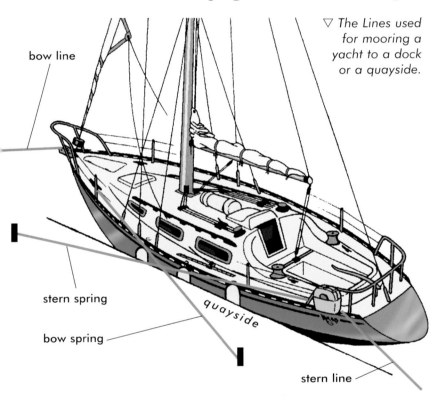

bow line

▽ The Lines used for mooring a yacht to a dock or a quayside.

stern spring

bow spring

quayside

stern line

## LIVING ABOARD

An important part of sailing in a yacht is that you are living aboard – even if it is only for a short time.

There may not be much space below in a small yacht, but it can be very snug and comfortable. However, if there is not much room, it does mean that all the crew have to be tidy and keep all their gear together. This is something that you have to learn. A yacht's small cabin is not quite like your room at home!

Living on board also means cooking and washing on the yacht, and again it is important to notice that it is all quite different from home. One of the key points to remember is that there is a strictly limited supply of fresh water. But if you keep your eyes open you will soon see how things are done.

Sadly there is no escape from washing up and you will still have to do your share afloat.

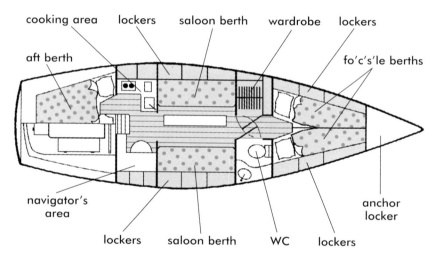

| cooking area | lockers | saloon berth | wardrobe | lockers |

aft berth

fo'c's'le berths

navigator's area

lockers    saloon berth    WC    lockers

anchor locker

△ Plan of the accommodation in a typical yacht.

## WHAT TO BRING WITH YOU

It is best to ask the skipper's advice beforehand. You do not want to bring too much because there may not be enough room to stow it. But it is important that you bring enough to keep yourself warm, dry and comfortable.

When you are dinghy sailing you will probably

get wet, but you can always go back to the club house to change into dry clothes. In a yacht it is different. You will need to take at least one change of clothes with you and enough of them to keep you really warm – even in summer.

One essential item is *shoes with non-slip soles*. This is more important on a yacht than in a dinghy because it can be dangerous moving around on a slippery deck without them, and regular trainers just do not work.

Because you need to keep warm and dry you will have to have some waterproof gear. If necessary, borrow what you need, but do not go without it. An extra towel to go around your neck is also useful as it stops water running down inside your waterproofs.

If you are going to be spending a night afloat you will need a sleeping bag. Some yachts provide them, but more often than not you will be asked to bring your own.

△ Cruising in a bigger boat may give you the opportunity to try your hand at navigation.

CHAPTER 16

# FLAGS

Vessels fly flags to show who they are and what they are doing. Until radio took their place, flags were used by ships to communicate with each other and with the shore.

△ The **Red Ensign** can be flown by any British vessel of any size.

△ The **Blue Ensign** is flown by vessels on government service (other than HM ships).

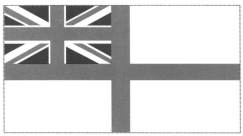

△ The **White Ensign** is flown by Royal Navy ships and by members of the Royal Yacht Squadron at Cowes on the Isle of Wight.

Racing flag

Hamble River Sailing Club

Poole Yacht Club

Royal Air Force Yacht Club

△ **Burgees**
Every yacht and sailing club has its own burgee, which, although a flag, is really the club badge. Any yacht belonging to that club will fly the burgee. It is also usually flown at the club flagstaff.

△ **International flag 'Q'** A yacht or vessel flying this flag indicates that she has just arrived from a foreign port and wants Customs clearance.

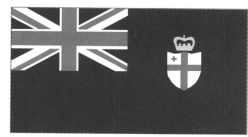

△ The **Blue Ensign** can also be flown by members of certain yacht clubs, who have this special privilege. The ensign flown by these clubs may sometimes be plain, or it may be 'defaced' with the club's insignia like the one above.

▽ A small coastal tanker flying a Red Ensign at the stern, a house flag at the masthead and the **International flag 'B'** at her port crosstree.

△ Dutch Ensign

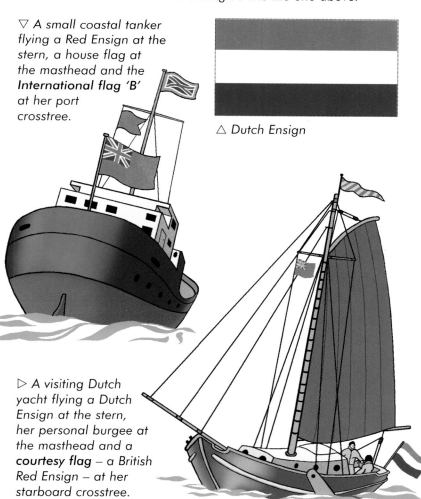

▷ A visiting Dutch yacht flying a Dutch Ensign at the stern, her personal burgee at the masthead and a **courtesy flag** – a British Red Ensign – at her starboard crosstree.

# DOUBLE QUIZ

## Quiz 1 - this is a simpler one.

1.  *What lines are used for hoisting sails?*
2.  *What is a cleat used for?*
3.  *What is a boat's transom?*
4.  *In a boat, what is the opposite to 'forward'?*
5.  *What is the main use for a figure of eight knot?*
6.  *How would you secure a tow from the safety boat?*
7.  *It is half past one and low water. At about what time will it be high water?*
8.  *What is the bottom, forward point of a sail called?*
9.  *What do the letters RYA stand for?*
10. *What is a boat's painter?*
11. *What is a burgee?*
12. *What kind of ensign does a Royal Navy ship fly?*
13. *What are you doing when you tack?*
14. *What is an offshore breeze?*
15. *Where can you usually find a weather forecast?*
16. *What is the opposite to 'leeward'?*
17. *In a river, where is the tide usually the strongest?*
18. *What is meant by 'pinching'?*
19. *What is meant by 'luffing'?*
20. *Which dinghies have sail letters C, E and W?*

**Answers:** 1. Halyards. 2. Securing the end of a line like a halyard. 3. The flat stern of a boat. 4. Aft. 5. To prevent the end of a line running through a block or lead. 6. Take a turn round the mast and hold the end. 7. About 7.40pm, just over six hours later. 8. The tack. 9. Royal Yachting Association. 10. Line used for securing bow of boat. 11. Triangular flag belonging to a yacht club. 12. White Ensign. 13. Altering course through the wind. 14. Wind blowing off the shore towards the water. 15. In the clubhouse, on the internet or on the radio. 16. Windward. 17. In the middle. 18. Trying to sail too close to the wind. 19. Turning the boat to head into the wind. 20. Cadet, Enterprise and Wayfarer.

## Quiz 2 - this one is a bit harder!

1. *What is the main difference between a buoyancy aid and a lifejacket?*

2. *When racing, what is an overlap?*

3. *How would you define the windward mark?*

4. *How are lighthouses and buoys equipped with a light shown on a chart?*

5. *What is the Beaufort Scale?*

6. *What is the difference between a hitch and a bend?*

7. *What is a sounding?*

8. *What is special about spring tides?*

9. *What have these boats got in common - Topper, Streaker, Optimist?*

10. *What is the purpose of a kicking strap?*

11. *You are racing. What does the shout 'Starboard!' mean?*

12. *What combination of colours is a cardinal buoy?*

13. *Describe the preparatory flag used at a race start.*

14. *What happens to the wind when it veers?*

15. *What is a bowline used for?*

16. *What is a 'general recall'?*

17. *What does 'sailing by the lee' mean?*

18. *What is meant by the 'range' of the tide?*

---

**Answers:** 1. A lifejacket must keep an unconscious person afloat, face up, and is normally inflatable. 2. When a boat has passed another's stern. 3. The upwind racing mark that you reach by tacking. 4. A purple blip. 5. Numerical scale for measuring wind strength. 6. A hitch secures a line to a bar, a post or a ring; a bend joins two lines together. 7. Depth of water shown on the chart. 8. Tides which are higher or lower than usual (just after new and full moon). 9. All have mainsail only. 10. To keep the boom down, and the mainsail in shape. 11. The other boat is on the starboard tack and you must give way if you are on port. 12. Black and yellow. 13. Blue with white centre (Blue Peter). 14. Its direction moves clockwise. 15. Making a loop at the end of a line. 16. When a number of boats are over the line at the start of a race, and the whole fleet is recalled. 17. Sailing with the wind right aft and on the wrong side of the mainsail. 18. The difference in height between low water (tide) and the next high water.

# SAILING TERMS & WORDS

**Most of these terms are to be found in this book. A few are new and may not apply to small boats, but all are worth knowing.**

**Abeam:** On the beam.
**Amidships:** In the middle of a boat or ship.
**Astern:** Towards the stern, or behind the boat.
**Athwartships:** From one side of the boat to the other.

**Batten:** A strip of wood or plastic used to keep a sail in shape.
**Beam:** The widest part of a boat's hull.
**Bear away:** To alter course away from the direction of the wind.
**Beat:** To sail to windward.
**Beaufort Scale:** Scale used for measuring wind strength.
**Block:** Type of pulley used afloat.
**Bowline:** Important knot for making a loop in a rope end.
**Burgee:** Triangular yacht club flag.

**Centreboard:** A hinged board that is lowered through the hull of a boat to provide a keel.
**Cleat:** A fitting for securing the tail end of a rope.
**Clew:** The bottom rear corner of a sail.
**Compass rose:** Compass shown on a chart from which you can plot courses and bearings.
**Cordage:** The collective term for ropes and lines.

**Dagger board:** A wooden board that can be raised or lowered in a dinghy to provide a keel.

**Draught:** The depth of a vessel below the waterline.

**Ebb** [tide]: The falling tide flowing towards the sea.
**Ensign:** A country's maritime flag.

**Fathom:** Unit of measurement (six feet) used for depth and measuring cordage. (Now obsolete, but still heard.)
**Fender:** A bumper, usually of inflatable plastic, put over the side of a boat to prevent damage when alongside a dock or another boat.
**Flood** [tide]: The flow of the rising tide.
**Foot:** The bottom edge of a sail.
**Forestay:** Rigging supporting the mast from forward.

**Go about:** See *Tack*.
**Gooseneck:** Fitting which secures the boom to the mast.
**Gunwhale** (pronounced *gunnal*): The top of the sides of a boat.
**Gybe:** To alter course when sailing, so that the stern passes through the wind.

**Halyard:** Line used to hoist a sail.
**Head:** The topmost corner of a sail.
**Heel:** *(1)* Leaning over to one side, as a boat does in the wind. *(2)* The bottom of the mast.

**Jib:** Triangular sail carried forward of the mast.

**Kicking strap:** A tackle used to haul the boom down and keep the shape in the mainsail.
**Knot:** (Nautical unit of speed.) One nautical mile (2,000 yards) per hour.

**Lee:** The side of a vessel away from the wind. *'In the lee'* means sheltered from the wind.
**Leech:** The rear edge of a sail.
**Log:** *(1)* A book in which a ship's activities and navigation details are recorded. *(2)* A device for measuring a vessel's speed and distance travelled.
**Luff up:** To alter a boat's course by turning up into the wind.

**Neap tides:** Tides with the smallest rise and fall.

**Overlap:** In racing, when one boat's bow has passed another's stern, both being on the same course.

**Painter:** Line attached to the bow of a dinghy to secure, or tow it.
**Pinching:** Pointing a boat too close to the wind, so that she will not sail properly.
**Point of sail:** The direction of sailing in relation to the wind.

**Range** [of the tide]: The difference in height, on any day, between high water and low water.
**Reach:** To sail with the wind on or slightly aft of the beam.
**Reef:** To reduce the area of sail when the wind increases in strength.
**Run:** To sail with the wind astern.

**Shackle:** A metal fitting for joining rigging or chain.
**Sheet:** A line used for controlling a sail.
**Shipshape:** Neat and tidy – as any boat should be.
**Shoal:** An area of shallow water.
**Shroud:** The rigging supporting the mast on either side.
**Slack water:** The period at high and low water when, for a short time, the tide hardly moves in either direction.
**Sounding:** The depth of water at a particular place.
**Spinnaker:** A light, very full sail carried forward of the mast when a boat is running before the wind (used especially when racing).
**Spring tides:** Tides with the greatest rise and fall.

**Tack:** *(1)* To alter course so that the bow passes through the wind. *(2)* The lower forward corner of a sail.
**Thwart:** A seat placed across the beam (width) of a boat.
**Topsides:** The outside area of the hull above the waterline.
**Transom:** The flat stern of a boat.
**Trapeze:** A seat or harness suspended from the mast head (used in more advanced dinghies), allowing the crew to sit out further to reducing excessive heeling.

**Veer:** *(1)* To let more line out. *(2)* The wind is said to veer when it changes direction in a clockwise direction.

**Whipping:** Twine bound round the end of a rope to prevent it from fraying.
**Windward:** Towards the wind, hence *windward* side.

# INDEX